D0575201

Festivals

Lantern Festival

by Rebecca Pettiford

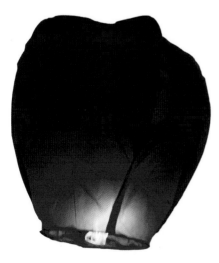

Bullfrog Books

Ideas for Parents and Teachers

Bullfrog Books let children practice reading informational text at the earliest reading levels. Repetition, familiar words, and photo labels support early readers.

Before Reading

- Discuss the cover photo. What does it tell them?

- Look at the picture glossary together. Read and discuss the words.

Read the Book

- "Walk" through the book and look at the photos. Let the child ask questions. Point out the photo labels.

- Read the book to the child, or have him or her read independently.

After Reading

- Prompt the child to think more. Ask: Have you ever celebrated the Lantern Festival? What sorts of things do you see during this festival?

Bullfrog Books are published by Jump!
5357 Penn Avenue South
Minneapolis, MN 55419
www.jumplibrary.com

Library of Congress Cataloging-in-Publication Data

Names: Pettiford, Rebecca, author.
Title: Lantern Festival / by Rebecca Pettiford.
Description: Minneapolis, Minnesota: Jump!, Inc., [2016] | Series: Festivals | Includes index.
Audience: Ages: 5-8. | Audience: Grades: K to Grade 3.
Identifiers: LCCN 2016025733 (print)
LCCN 2016033973 (ebook)
ISBN 9781620315330 (hard cover: alk. paper)
ISBN 9781620315873 (paperback)
ISBN 9781624964879 (e-book)
Subjects: LCSH: Festivals—Taiwan—Juvenile literature. | Lanterns—Taiwan—Social life and customs—Juvenile literature.
Classification: LCC GT4883.5.A2 P48 2016 (print)
LCC GT4883.5.A2 (ebook) | DDC 394.26951249—dc23
LC record available at https://lccn.loc.gov/2016025733

Editor: Kirsten Chang
Book Designer: Leah Sanders
Photo Researcher: Leah Sanders

Photo Credits: All photos by Shutterstock except: Alamy, 8–9, 23bl; Getty, 4, 5, 6–7, 9, 14–15, 18, 23tl, 24; iStock, 1; Johnson76/Shutterstock.com, 16–17; Tappasan Phurisamrit/Shutterstock.com, 19.

Printed in the United States of America at Corporate Graphics in North Mankato, Minnesota.

Table of Contents

Sky Lights

It is the end
of Chinese
New Year.

In Taiwan, the moon is full.

The Lantern Festival is here!

We make lanterns.

We hang them up.

Riddles hang from some lanterns.

We try to answer one.

Wei gets it right.

He wins a prize!

We go to the temple.

We see red lanterns.
Red is a lucky color.

We eat tangyuan.

Yum!

They look like
full moons.

tangyuan

It is night.

We go out.

Wow! Look at the lanterns!

Some look like animals.

Look! A dragon!

We write wishes on lanterns.

18

We let the lanterns go.

They rise.

They fill the sky.

The Lantern
Festival is fun!

Festival Lanterns

red lanterns

animal lanterns

sky lanterns

riddle lanterns

Picture Glossary

Chinese New Year
The Chinese festival marking the start of the lunar year.

Taiwan
An island off the coast of China.

festival
A special time when people gather to celebrate something.

tangyuan
Rice balls filled with sweet paste.

riddles
Tricky questions presented as a problem to be solved.

temple
A building where people go to pray.

Index

To Learn More

Learning more is as easy as 1, 2, 3.

1) Go to www.factsurfer.com

2) Enter "LanternFestival" into the search box.

3) Click the "Surf" button to see a list of websites.

With factsurfer.com, finding more information is just a click away.